THE GHOSTLY TALES OF ALABAMA

To Samuel, the latest addition to our family.

Published by Arcadia Children's Books
A Division of Arcadia Publishing
Charleston, SC
www.arcadiapublishing.com

Copyright © 2023 by Arcadia Children's Books
All rights reserved

Spooky America is a trademark of Arcadia Publishing, Inc.

First published 2023

Manufactured in the United States

ISBN 978-1-4671-9729-8

Library of Congress Control Number: 2022932233

All images used courtesy of Shutterstock.com; p. 6 Malachi Jacobs/Shutterstock.com;
p. 34 NatalieSchorr/Shutterstock.com; p. 49-50 JNix/Shutterstock.com; p. 62 Stephen
Reeves/Shutterstock.com; p. 76-77 Darryl Brooks/Shutterstock.com

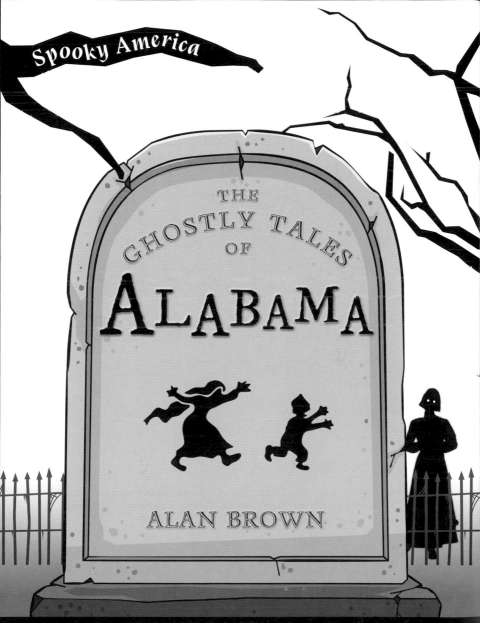

Spooky America

THE
GHOSTLY TALES
OF
ALABAMA

ALAN BROWN

Adapted from *Haunted Alabama* by Alan Brown

arcadia
CHILDREN'S BOOKS

TABLE OF CONTENTS & MAP KEY

Welcome to Spooky Alabama!

Alabama is a state with beaches in the south, mountains in the north, and hundreds of years of history in between. Some of the oldest universities in the nation are in Alabama, and so are some of the grandest old houses you'll ever see. There is art, music, theater, and lots more to love!

Like any place with a long history, Alabama has some dark sides, too. In the antebellum ("pre-war") years, many thousands of people of color were enslaved here. During the Civil War in the 1860s, people were killed and buildings destroyed. In the years that followed, many people struggled to make sense of the changes they saw after slavery was outlawed: sadly, some even took justice into their own hands, including "lynch mobs" (violent gangs that targeted African Americans) that condemned their victims to death by hanging with no trial, often facing no consequences. It was

a frightening, difficult time—you might not be surprised to hear that some of Alabama's most famous ghost stories stem from these troubled years.

Other stories arose from tales of tragic accidents or lost love. Some took root when illness ran rampant through out the country, death taking loved ones all too quickly. Some legends found homes in abandoned buildings, which just have a way of feeling spooky! There are as many ghost stories as there are stars over Alabama . . . but are they true? Join us for a tour through some of the state's most haunted places and decide for yourself!

Kendall Manor

Haunted Houses

CEDARHURST MANSION, HUNTSVILLE

In folklore, ghosts return for a variety of reasons. Sometimes they return to warn the living, complete unfinished business, reveal the location of hidden treasure, or protest the way they died. In the story of Cedarhurst Mansion, one restless spirit seems to have been asking for a little help with her "home."

In 1823, a wealthy businessman named Stephen Ewing and his wife, Mary Carter

Ewing, built Cedarhurst Mansion. The home was large and lovely, with a stately portico entrance (a grand, covered entryway supported by decorative columns). It sat high on a hill beside a grove of cedar trees, which gave the home its name. In 1837, Mary's sister Sally Carter came to visit. She stayed with the family for several weeks before becoming deathly ill. She died on November 28, 1837, and was buried in the little family cemetery behind the house.

Many years later, in 1919, a seventeen-year-old relative named Stephen Scott, from Germantown, Pennsylvania, came to Cedarhurst for a house party with some family members.

During his first night in the house, the rumbling of a terrible thunderstorm woke him. Blinking his eyes, the young man was startled to see the image of a beautiful girl in a white dress standing outside his window. He lay back down and pulled the covers over his head. A few seconds later, he heard a female voice cry, "Help me! Help me!" At first, Stephen was terrified, but after a moment, his curiosity got the best of him and he sat up from underneath the covers. There, standing by his bedside, was the same pretty girl. "The wind blew my tombstone over," she said. "Please set it upright." Then she vanished.

The next morning, Stephen rushed to the dining room, anxious to tell his family what had happened during the night. But when he came to the end of his tale, the family only laughed. Even his youngest cousin declared, "You must have been dreaming! There's no such thing as ghosts." Stephen insisted the visit was real, so the family decided to go to the backyard cemetery and take a look. Sure enough, Sally Carter's tombstone was lying on the ground! No one made fun of Stephen after that.

In the decades that followed, the little graveyard had many more visitors: Local teenagers would sneak in and dare each other to lie down on Sally Carter's grave. In 1982, the Ewing graves were dug up and moved to Maple Hurst Cemetery, where they were buried in unmarked graves so that they would no longer be disturbed. Hopefully, Sally Carter is resting in peace at last.

BLUFF HALL, DEMOPOLIS

Another home named for its location is the two-story Bluff Hall, which sits on a bluff (or cliff) overlooking the Tombigbee River. It was built in 1832 as a wedding gift to Sarah Glover and Francis Lyon from Sarah's parents. In the 1840s, the couple renovated the house, adding wide, rectangular columns to the front and new rooms to the back. It was just one of the homes Sarah and Francis owned: They spent most of their time on their various plantations, so Bluff Hall served as their townhouse—a place to stay when they wanted to sample the excitement and variety of city life, or when Francis's work as a lawyer and politician brought them to Demopolis.

Francis and Sarah had seven children (six girls and one boy), and for the next 75 years, members of their family continued living in the house. Later, it was converted into apartments, but it has since been restored as a historic home where visitors can get a glimpse into the way people lived almost two centuries ago.

Following the restoration, local resident and Demopolis Chamber of Commerce president, Kathy Leverett, spent the night in Bluff Hall with her daughter and some of her daughter's friends. There were rumors about spirits in the house, and Kathy and the girls were curious to find out if any of the ghostly tales were true. Sure enough, just before bedtime, everyone heard what sounded like someone jumping rope. The sound persisted for a while, stopped, and started up again. When the noises quieted down (and the group quieted their nerves!), Kathy and the girls finally went to sleep. But a little while later, Kathy awakened to the same mysterious sound. Quietly, she left the group of sleeping girls and tiptoed up the stairs to investigate. She had almost reached the top of the stairs when, suddenly, she sensed that someone was standing next to her. She looked down and saw beside her a young boy, who looked to be about eight years old. Instead of experiencing fear, she felt sorry for the child: From his sad expression, Kathy sensed he was looking for his mother.

She headed back down the stairs, thinking the little boy would follow her. However, when she reached the bottom and turned around, he was gone. The next morning, as Kathy and the girls were leaving Bluff Hall, she saw the little figure once more. Only this time, he was gazing out the window toward the road . . . the same wistful expression on his face.

Some think the boy at Bluff Hill was the ghost of little Leonidas Mecklenburg Polk, or "Merk." Around 1869, an eight-year-old boy by that name had come to Bluff Hill to spend time with his grandparents while his family prepared for a new baby back home in New York. Tragically, Merk soon became sick with scarlet fever. He must have longed to see his mother—but she was not able to come to him

before he died. He was buried in the family plot in Riverside Cemetery without being able to gaze into his mother's face one last time. Perhaps this is why he still shows up at Bluff Hall, waiting for her to come back for him.

THE CLEVELAND HOUSE, SUGGSVILLE

If we make a promise, we should keep it, right? That's what Stephen Cleveland always tried to do for his son. Those who have heard hoofbeats at Cleveland House think he might still be trying.

As a young man in 1849, South Carolina–born Stephen Cleveland joined thousands of fortune hunters seeking treasure in the California Gold Rush. We don't know if he struck it rich or not. What we do know is that he came to Alabama ready to settle down. He married eighteen-year-old Eliza Davis Creagh, started a career as a politician and state senator, and, in 1860, built a large, L-shaped house, with verandas—or covered porches—that wrapped around the building. The house was soon filled with family, including Stephen and Eliza, their children Lillian and Walter, and Eliza's younger brother.

Stephen was a devoted family man who doted on his children. He loved taking Walter for rides on his horse, trotting between the long rows of cotton fields or galloping down the road. One day, on a whim, he and four-year-old Walter rode the horse up the front steps of the house, around the porch, and down the north steps. Walter begged to do it again, but his mother put a stop to that! Walter was just as devoted to Stephen: When Stephen once traveled to Montgomery without telling his son, the little boy was so upset that his father promised never to leave again without saying goodbye.

Sadly, the next goodbye was their last. Stephen had lived in his beautiful home for only a year before the Civil War erupted. In March 1861, Stephen organized a company of cavalry (soldiers on horseback) called the "Suggsville Greys," and left in April to join the war. On the day he left, he made sure to tell Walter goodbye. He then picked up the boy, set him on the horse, and rode around the porch. Setting Walter down, Stephen promised he would take his son for another "porch ride" when he returned.

Unfortunately, Stephen wasn't able to keep his promise. Walter died in July 1861, just a few days before his fifth birthday, while his father was away. Understandably, Stephen was devastated. He survived the war and came home as promised, but poor Walter's porch ride was never to be . . . at least not in his lifetime.

Today, the Cleveland House is used as a hunting lodge. For years, members of the hunting club claim to have heard the clip-clop of a horse's hooves climbing up the north steps, racing around the veranda, and charging down the east steps. When people hear these ghostly sounds, they say that Stephen Cleveland's ghost is taking his son, Walter, on that final ride.

Gaineswood, Demopolis

In 1834, Elizabeth and Nathan Whitfield moved from North Carolina to West Alabama to start a cotton plantation. Cotton was a popular and profitable business at that time—especially in Alabama, where the growing season was long, the soil was rich, and slave labor was considered acceptable by many. Their business may have been a success, but after three of their twelve children died, the Whitfields decided it was time to move again.

They began construction of a grand new house in Demopolis, renting a nearby cabin to live in until the house was complete. With plans for eighteen rounded columns, fourteen square pillars, and three grand porches, "Gaineswood" was to be the most splendid plantation house in all of Alabama. But before it was complete, *another* shadow passed over the family: Elizabeth Whitfield, herself, died! By the mid-1850s, Nathan and his younger children were living in the still-unfinished mansion. Rather than send his daughters away to school, Nathan hired a teacher and governess, Miss Carter, who came from Virginia to live with them. After a few months, Miss Carter became homesick, so Nathan arranged for her sister, Evelyn, to come to Gaineswood as well. Evelyn proved to be an invaluable addition to the family. On cold winter evenings, she played piano while Nathan played the bagpipes, and the children sang along. The formerly gloomy mansion became a place of joy.

Soon, Evelyn found even more joy: She fell in love with a young officer from a nearby French settlement. The romance blossomed quickly, and within a few weeks, the happy couple had plans to marry. Alas, the bad luck surrounding the Whitfield family struck again. One fateful day, as they talked in the garden at

Gaineswood, the pair got into an argument. In a fit of rage, the officer removed the engagement ring from Evelyn's finger and threw it into the bushes. Some say that it was pneumonia that led to Evelyn's death soon after; others believe she died of a broken heart.

Evelyn's dying wish was to be buried in her family's plot in Virginia. Nathan had agreed on the spot. However, the winter weather made the roads to Virginia wet, muddy, and impassible. To preserve Evelyn's body until it could be moved in the spring, it was placed in a pine box sealed with resin and stored in a cool space in the basement. Before long, the servants reported hearing footsteps walking up and down the basement stairs when there was nobody there. Some claimed to have heard phantom fingers playing the piano at night.

Everyone breathed a sigh of relief when the roads finally dried up, and Evelyn's body was buried in her native Virginia. They hoped that the eerie noises would go away. To their dismay, the noises continued well into the next century! One woman recalls a sleepover at Gaineswood in the 1940s: During the night, she and her friend were awakened by the sound of old-fashioned songs being played on the piano. They went downstairs, but no one was there. That is, no one they could see.

KENDALL MANOR, EUFAULA

The town of Eufaula is known throughout Alabama for its large number of beautifully preserved homes from before the Civil War. One of these mansions, Kendall Manor, was built by James Turner Kendall, a wealthy cotton merchant, in 1850. Built to impress, Kendall Manor features ornate columns and a wraparound porch skirted with rosebushes, and a white belvedere (tower) atop the roof, setting it apart from neighboring homes. Kendall Manor is also distinctive because of its ghost story.

After the Kendall family moved into the grand mansion, they hired a nursemaid named Annie to look after the children. Annie was a large woman who wore a stern expression and kept a close eye on the kids—especially the boys, who seemed to be the primary troublemakers. Many years after Annie died, one of James Turner Kendall's great-great-grandsons was racing his tricycle on the porch outside the house when he glanced up at a window and saw a frowning woman in an old-fashioned dress; hands on her hips; dark, angry eyes seeming to stare right

through him. With a shudder, the boy realized that he *could* see right through her! Alarmed, he lost control of his tricycle and veered off the porch and into the rose bushes below. He suffered a few scratches on his arms and legs, but his injuries were nothing compared to the bad dreams that disturbed his sleep for the next couple of weeks. Annie seems to be one of those dedicated caregivers still on the job, even though they'd passed away years before.

LAKEWOOD, LIVINGSTON

Across the street from the University of West Alabama stands Lakewood, one of the oldest houses in Livingston. The grand portico on the front of the three-story house features a second-floor main entrance, accessed by a pair of iron staircases. This second floor was the main living floor, with bedrooms below and above—a relatively unusual setup when Lakewood was built nearly two hundred years ago. Seven generations of Joseph Lake's descendants would go on to live here.

It is not surprising that a house as old as Lakewood has given rise to ghost stories, but the consistency of the eyewitness reports is striking—specifically, the distinctive shirt that appears in almost every story. Here is one example from the 1940s: Early one morning, Eloise Boyd was sitting in the kitchen with her friend Bradford Jones, a grandson of the owners, when she saw a man in a plaid shirt walk past the kitchen window. Eloise pointed to the man and asked, "Who is that?" Bradford looked out the window and replied, "Oh, that's just our ghost." Then he went back to eating his breakfast.

Twenty years later, Bradford's daughter Olivia was making the bed in a third-floor guest room when, out of the corner of her eye, she saw a man in a plaid shirt walk past the doorway. At first, she assumed it was a family member and exclaimed, "Oh, you scared me!" When no one answered back, Olivia realized that she had just seen the family ghost. She dashed down the stairs, raced out the front door, and sat shaking on the top steps until her father came home. When he arrived, Olivia announced, "I'm not going back up there with that ghost in the room!"

In 2009, Olivia's daughter, Sydney, discovered that the family ghost had a mischievous side. A friend of hers named Tyler stopped off at Lakewood after football practice to shower. Using the key she loaned him, Tyler entered the empty house and walked to the bathroom. He had not been showering for long when the lights started flickering on and off. At first, it did not bother him—after all, it was an old house with old wiring. But when the lights continued to flicker several more times, Tyler became concerned. He got dressed as fast as he could, and, like Sydney's mom years before, sat on the front steps to wait for the family. He could hardly wait to tell them about his scary experience inside the house.

The Lake family has gotten used to having ghostly interruptions in their daily routines now and then. Nevertheless, more than half a century later, Olivia *still* refuses to walk up the stairs to the third floor. This could be why she has only seen the man in the plaid shirt once.

STURDIVANT HALL, SELMA

The historic house museum now called Sturdivant Hall was once known as the "Watts-Parkman-Gillman House"—named for the three different families that owned it in just its first fifteen years. The first owner, Colonel Edward T. Watts, oversaw the building of the six-thousand-square-foot house, hiring European artisans for fine finishes such as detailed plasterwork, Italian marble, and a spiral staircase leading to a rooftop cupola. Banker John McGee Parkman and his family bought the house in 1864; in 1870, Emile Gillman took ownership, and his family lived in the home for nearly a century. Although each left his mark, it was John Parkman who seems to have left a haunting presence behind, perhaps tied to his own dramatic end.

As president of the First National Bank of Selma, John Parkman was responsible for safeguarding the money of his clients—one of whom was the U.S. government. Unfortunately, the bank lost a great deal of money when the price of cotton crashed after the Civil War. In 1867, Alabama's military governor accused Watts of stealing the money and imprisoned him at Castle Morgan in Old Cahaba.

Parkman's friends concocted a scheme to help him escape. On May 23, 1867, they organized a parade in front of the jail to distract the guards. While the guards watched the singers and jugglers, John Parkman snuck out and began climbing the prison wall, trying to reach the river on the other side. What happened next is still a mystery. In one version of the story, guards shot and killed Parkman as he dived into the water. In another version, he was able to dive into the river without being shot, but he was crushed under a steamboat's paddlewheel. In yet another variant, one of his friends had helped him embezzle (steal) the bank's money, but then shot and killed John to protect himself and make sure nobody could ever find out what he had done. The most sensational story of all deals not with where Parkman died . . . but where he turned up afterward.

Soon after Sturdivant Hall opened as a house museum, staff and visitors reported seeing the ghost of John Parkman in the cupola (small lookout) on top of the house and in his daughters' upstairs bedroom. Others say they have heard his restless spirit walking around upstairs or seen doors opening and closing on their own.

Parkman's ghost may be responsible for the scariest incident ever reported in the mansion. One day, an exterminator arrived to spray for pests, carrying his equipment upstairs for what he thought would be a routine appointment. After a few minutes, he came running down the stairs with a terrified look on his face. He told the museum staff that somebody had pushed him onto the floor ... then he ran out of the house so fast he left all his equipment upstairs!

The ghosts of Parkman's children have also appeared, staring out of a second-floor window. In 2001, some schoolchildren were standing in the children's room, where a large painting sat on an easel. Suddenly, the painting seemed to jump from the easel onto the floor, shattering the frame. The students were convinced that Parkman's daughters pushed the picture off the easel to get their attention.

McCARTNEY TERRACE

Auburn Hall

CHAPTER 2

Haunted Colleges and Universities

ATHENS STATE UNIVERSITY (McCANDLESS HALL), ATHENS

Sometimes, the spirits in ghost legends form strong connections to the places where they enjoyed their greatest triumph. The ghost of McCandless Hall at Athens State University fits into this category. In 1914, not long after McCandless Hall was dedicated, the school held a special concert in the auditorium. A promising young musician named Abigail

Burns performed that night, singing an aria from the opera *La Traviata*. The audience was thrilled: They showered Abigail with thunderous applause, and a little girl walked across the stage to give her a bouquet of long-stemmed roses. Abigail stood on the stage, bowing and blowing kisses to the audience. Then, with tears streaming down her cheeks, Abigail vowed that she would return to McCandless Hall someday.

Outside, clouds had been building up during the concert. By the time Abigail exited the building and rushed inside the waiting carriage, rain was coming down in torrents. The story goes that as the carriage crossed a bridge over a gorge, lighting streaked across the sky. The frightened horse reared up and the carriage plunged to the rocks below. Both Abigail and the driver were killed.

According to the stories shared by Athens State students on dark and stormy nights, Abigail Burns kept her promise. For over a century, the specter of a young woman with long, blonde hair has been seen standing in a third-floor window in McCandless Hall. Cradled in her arms is a bouquet of long-stemmed roses. Occasionally, the figure appears surrounded by an eerie light.

Of course, not everyone on campus believes that the ghost of Abigail Burns is real. In 1997, a professor at the University researched the legend and found no evidence that an opera singer named Abigail Burns even sang at McCandless Hall in 1914, or of any accident involving a carriage and the gorge. Not surprisingly, his findings have not discouraged students from talking about the ghost of

Abigail Burns. After all, there may be plenty of facts in the classroom ... but when it comes to spooky faces in upstairs windows, seeing is believing.

Auburn University (University Chapel), Auburn

University Chapel is the second oldest building at Auburn University. During the Civil War, it was used as a field hospital for wounded Confederate soldiers. One day, a British cavalryman named Sydney Grimlett was shot in the leg while fighting with the Confederate Sixth Virginia Calvary during the Atlanta Campaign. By the time the surgeon on duty was able to tend to Sydney, an infection had set in, and the leg had to be amputated (cut off) to prevent the spread of the disease. Despite the surgery, Sydney Grimlett died just a few hours later.

In the years that followed, University Chapel served a number of different purposes: it held classes, housed the YMCA, and by 1926, a theatrical group named the Auburn Players had begun performing plays in the old church. Some students and faculty say the hauntings began shortly after the performance of a popular mid-19th-century English play. Supposedly, the ghost of Sydney Grimlett made his presence known by causing props to malfunction, moving scenery on stage, whistling in the attic, and stamping with his one remaining foot. Some even believe the ghost was responsible for a green glow that suddenly appeared over the ceiling during a production of Eugene O'Neill's play *Long Day's Journey into Night*.

The Auburn Players learned to live with the mischievous ghost,

but they didn't officially know its identity until a group of young actors sat inside the darkened theater one night with a Ouija board—a wooden board with letters printed on it that people use to contact the spirit world. To use it, people place their hands on a pointer and ask the spirits questions. Sometimes, nothing happens. Other times … the pointer moves back and forth across the board, spelling out words that form messages. When the actors placed their hands on the Ouija board that night and asked the spirits to name their ghost, they watched in astonishment as the pointer moved over the letters and slowly spelled out:

"S-Y-D-N-E-Y-G-R-I-M-L-E-T-T." Were the spirits really guiding their hands? Or were the hopeful actors simply remembering old stories as they, themselves, spelled out his name? Either way, the Auburn Players embraced their ghost's identity, even naming an award given to the most outstanding theater student "The Sydney Award." Following the re-dedication of the University Chapel, the sightings of Sydney's ghost died down. Some students believe, however, that Sydney moved into the Pect Theatre, where—to this day—strange, unexplainable disturbances occasionally occur.

SPRING HILL COLLEGE, MOBILE

Spring Hill College is Alabama's oldest Catholic school, founded in 1830 by Bishop Michael Porter and originally staffed by two priests and four seminarians. Initially intended for students under twelve years old, the school expanded quickly, and within two years, it included a high school and college. Over the past two hundred years, many Jesuit priests have left their mark on Spring Hill—both during their lifetimes and, so the story goes, even *beyond*.

Those priests from generations past are never far away: Unlike most colleges, Spring Hill has its own graveyard, with the remains of all the priests who have taught there. Many students walking around the graveyard at night claim to have seen the figure of a black hooded monk walking around the tombstones.

Another Spring Hill ghost story is set in a far less spooky setting: a math classroom in Quinlan Hall. Here, a priest named Father Mueller taught mathematics for many years. He was a popular teacher, remembered fondly by many students and known for a particular tradition: Toward the end of each semester, he put what he called "the unsolvable math problem" on the board. Anyone who solved the problem would receive extra credit. Many tried, but few succeeded. The problem was so difficult that only the best students earned the extra credit.

After Father Mueller died, he was replaced by a young Jesuit priest who decided to keep up the tradition of the unsolvable math problem. Toward the end of his first semester as Father Mueller's replacement, the priest wrote the problem on the board and instructed his students to take it home and try to solve it.

The next morning, the priest asked the students if anyone had solved the problem. Everyone sat motionless at their desks. Then, after a minute or so, one student raised his hand. To the teacher's surprise, it was a student who was barely passing the course. Based on his work so far, there was no way he could have solved the extra-credit problem.

To everybody's surprise, the young man walked to the front of the classroom, picked up a piece of chalk, and began writing. For the next minute or two, he filled the blackboard with complex calculations. The young priest walked to the front of the room and inspected the student's work. With a broad smile, he asked the student how he managed to get the correct answer. He was stunned by the student's explanation.

The young man said he had stayed up late the night before, trying to solve the problem but found it impossible. He was just about to give up and go to bed when the door to his dorm room opened, and an old priest walked in and offered to help. Sitting next to the student at his desk, the old priest told him how to solve the problem. When the student had finished telling his story, the young priest asked him to describe his midnight visitor. His description matched a picture the priest had seen of Father Mueller *exactly*. Since then, the old math professor's ghost has been seen many times, almost always in the math department.

THE UNIVERSITY OF ALABAMA
(JASON'S SHRINE), TUSCALOOSA

During the Civil War, the University of Alabama was home to a Corps of Cadets, which trained officers for the Confederate Army. So many officers graduated from the University of Alabama that it became known as "The West Point of the South," and was considered a military target by Union forces. So, on April 4, 1865, when Union General John T. Croxton's force of 1,500 cavalrymen attacked Tuscaloosa, Alabama, they destroyed not only the city's factories and warehouses, but also most of the buildings on the university's campus.

The story goes that while most of the cadets were fighting Croxton's men on the outskirts of town, two of them decided they would remain to defend the campus. They walked past rows of burning buildings until finally stopping at the sentry box, called the Little Round House, which had escaped destruction. One of the cadets entered the sentry box with his rifle in his hands and sat down in a darkened corner at the back of the building. Meanwhile, his friend walked over to the nearby library, which was engulfed in flames. He approached a group of three Union soldiers—a burly-looking sergeant and two boyish-looking privates—and watched them throw books into the fire. The sergeant noticed him and asked, "Boy, do you know where we can get our hands on some whiskey?"

Nodding his head nervously, the cadet replied, "Yes, sir. The cadets keep their whiskey in the sentry box." The young man led the three thirsty soldiers to the little white building where his friend was waiting. The cadet threw open the door and stepped aside.

You can imagine their surprise when they were gunned down by the shadowy figure sitting on the floor.

Long after the Civil War ended, the Little Round House became a meeting place for a men's honor society called the "Jasons." Today, it is known as the Jason's Shrine, and is the official memorial for all of the honor societies in the university's history—and the unofficial memorial to one not-so-honorable search party. Students still stop to press their ears against the door, hoping to hear the ghosts of the three Union soldiers rummaging around, looking for their barrel of whiskey.

University of Montevallo
(Old Main), Montevallo

Established in 1896 as the Alabama Girls' Industrial School, the University of Montevallo is believed by many to be the *most* haunted university in the entire state. Students and faculty agree that the most haunted building on campus is the Main Residence Hall ("Old Main"). The creepiest ghost stories always have a basis in fact, and this is certainly true of the legend of Condie Cunningham.

An article published in the local newspaper reported that on February 4, 1908, a student named Condie was in her room on the third floor, making hot chocolate over a little flame to ward off the chill of the night air. Somehow, she accidentally knocked over the flame, setting her nightgown ablaze. Instead of dropping to the floor and rolling around, which

University of Montevallo

is what you are supposed to do if you catch on fire, she ran screaming down the hallway, fanning the flames that had engulfed her body. She had not run very far before collapsing in a heap at the top of the stairs, where she died.

Students living in Old Main have been sharing stories about Condie Cunningham's unquiet spirit for over a century. They feel a chilly breeze blowing down the hallway, even when the windows are closed. They observe doors and windows that have opened by themselves. They notice places where the carpet is *rippling*, as if an invisible being is walking across it. Some students say they have heard Condie screaming in the shower room, and others report hearing a spectral voice pleading, "Help me!" in the hallway. For years, students have claimed that on the anniversary of her death, Condie's ghost can be seen running down the hallway, screaming.

Even today, Montevallo students are afraid to stay in Condie's room. There have simply been too many reports of students waking to the sounds of her talking at night—and of her screams. The university even removed the door to Condie's room after some students said they could see a screaming face in the grain of wood. It's been stored in the basement ever since.

If *you* go down to that basement and see the door for yourself, you might notice something that kind of looks like a face . . . or you may just be caught up in the spooky legend!

University of North Alabama (Off-Campus Bookstore), Florence

Most College or university ghost stories deal with college-age students, around eighteen to twenty-two years old. The ghosts haunting the Off-Campus Bookstore are an exception. The bookstore is housed in what was once a private residence built in the early 1900s by a wealthy merchant. Although the merchant and his wife had plenty of money and a beautiful home, what they really wanted was a child. The couple tried for years to have a baby and had almost given up when little Molly was born.

Molly's parents spoiled her shamelessly—especially her father, who brought her a little present every day when he returned from work. One day, he opened the front door, and Molly ran up to him, expecting to be given candy or a small toy. Keeping both hands behind his back, her father said, "I'm sorry. I forgot to get you something this time." Molly was not convinced; she ran behind his back and grabbed a box that he was holding in his hands. It was approximately the size of a shoe box. She knew it wasn't shoes, though, because it had holes punched in the sides, and something seemed to be moving around in it. Molly removed the lid, and there was a tiny puppy.

Molly and her new pet hit it off immediately and soon became inseparable. One hot August day, Molly and her dog had been playing outside for about an hour when she decided to take a bath. She was walking slowly up the stairs when her little dog began scratching and biting the back of her legs. Molly's mother heard her screams and rushed up the stairs. Scooping the little girl into her arms, she carried her upstairs to the bathroom to wash her

wounds. Unfortunately, it turned out that Molly's puppy was sick with rabies. The little girl became infected and died in great pain.

In the next several decades, the house had several different owners. In the 1970s, the University of North Alabama purchased the old home and turned it into a fraternity house. The fraternity boys needed a large room where they could hold meetings, so they knocked down a couple of walls. Folklorists and experts in the paranormal claim that making any structural changes to a house "stirs up the spirits," and this seems to be what happened. After dinner

one night, the boys gathered in the great room to talk. After a while, they heard a dog barking upstairs ... but when they ran up the steps, there was no sign of a dog anywhere. At night, they began hearing the weeping of a little girl. Wiping sleep from their eyes, the boys searched for the little girl, but she was nowhere to be found.

That fall, the homecoming queen and her court were sitting on the balcony of the fraternity house, watching the homecoming parade. One of the young ladies noticed a little girl walking along the side of the house.

Because the child was wearing an old-fashioned dress, the girl assumed she had wandered away from one of the parade floats and was lost. She exited the house as fast as she could and took off after the little girl, who was just rounding the corner of the house. By the time she got there, the child was gone.

In 1970, the fraternity boys hired a man to look after the fraternity house while they were gone for summer vacation. Late one afternoon, the man was walking down the sidewalk with a bag of groceries in his arms. As he approached the house, he noticed a little girl in an old-fashioned dress sitting on the curb with a little black dog. He asked the girl if she was lost, and she replied, "Oh, no, sir. I live here." She then got up from the curb, and she and the dog walked into the house—right through the closed front door.

UNIVERSITY OF WEST ALABAMA, LIVINGSTON

The University of West Alabama started out as Livingston Female Academy when it was founded in 1835. Webb Hall, Livingston's first dormitory, was built in 1895—but not long after, it suffered two catastrophic fires: It burned down in 1909 and was rebuilt in 1911, then burned down again in 1914 and was rebuilt in 1915. The latter still stands today and has served as administrative offices since 1970s. Some of the staff who work there, however, sense that one of the fires left behind at least *one* restless spirit.

The first reported sighting in Webb Hall occurred in 1993. George Snow was working late in his office on the second floor. He was the only person in the building. Around 9:00 p.m., he left his office for a drink of water. As he walked down the corridor to the main hallway, George suddenly smelled the old-fashioned fragrance of lilac perfume. Then he caught a glimpse of a young woman walking down the hallway, wearing a late 19th-century dress with petticoats. Shivers ran up his spine. George told himself that he had done enough work that evening; he returned to his office, packed up his briefcase, and went home.

George is the only person who has seen the ghost in Webb Hall, but he is not the only person who has made the ghost's acquaintance. In 2006, a university employee named Lawson Edmonds returned to his office on the second floor of Webb with his daughter and two of her friends during Christmas break. They were in the same stretch of hallway where George Snow had been when all of them smelled lilac perfume. Lawson had smelled the perfume before but had not told his daughter until that particular afternoon. "The smell usually appears when the building has been closed for a while, like on weekends or during breaks," Lawson said. "When this happens, the hair rises up on my arms." In 2022, Terri Biglane was standing outside the door of her office when she, too, detected the unmistakable scent of lilac perfume. "When I smelled that perfume, George Snow's experience years before immediately came to mind," she said.

Sloss Furnaces

CHAPTER 3

Haunted Buildings

SLOSS FURNACES, BIRMINGHAM

The iron industry came to Birmingham in 1881, when work began on Sloss Furnaces. The factory's two state-of-the-art blast furnaces (named Alice 1 and Alice 2, after Sloss's daughter) could produce a daily total of eighty tons of "pig iron" (iron that has been liquified in super-hot temperatures to remove minerals). The iron was then shipped to Louisville, Cincinnati, Cleveland, and Chicago.

Birmingham was ideally suited for a new factory because of the large number of men looking for work—and Sloss would provide plenty of it. But work in a foundry meant hot, dangerous labor. No one knows for certain how many workers were maimed or killed in industrial accidents at Sloss Furnaces in the decade they were open. Many of these deaths have become stories passed down through generations.

One of the unfortunate workers who met a tragic end was Theophilus Calvin Jowers, who left his father's plantation after the Civil War and went looking for factory work in Jefferson County. After marrying Sarah Latham in 1870, he worked at the Cahaba Iron Works, then the Oxmoor Furnace. But his dream was to work as a foundryman at Sloss, which was known as the best ironworks in town. In the spring of 1887, that dream came true when Jowers began work at Sloss as an assistant foundryman (supervisor). Sarah wished he would find a safer job, but her husband would say, "Don't worry, the furnace is my friend. As long as there's a furnace standing in this county, I'll be there."

On September 10, 1887, Sarah's worst fears came true. Jowers and a team of workers were assigned the task of replacing the bell-shaped dome on Alice No. 1. First, they would dispose of the old dome by melting it down in the tank. As the men prepared to lower the old dome into the molten metal, Jowers was walking along the rim of the tank, calling out orders. Suddenly, he lost his balance and plummeted into molten iron below. Those who witnessed the tragic accident surmised that Jowers probably didn't feel much pain: He was incinerated in just a few seconds. Several workers standing at the top of the furnace attached a long metal pole to a large piece of sheet metal in an attempt to retrieve some of Jowers's remains. All they could recover were his head, intestines, two hip bones, and a few ashes.

The ironworkers at Sloss Furnaces took care of their own. Sarah Jowers was able to make a living selling sandwiches to her husband's former co-workers. Before long, she heard some of her customers talking about an apparition that seemed to keep an eye on things from an upper stairway, just like a foundryman would do.

By the 1920s, the ghost seemed to have moved across the street to Alice 2. In 1927, Jowers's son, John, was driving his Model-T Ford over the viaduct near Alice 2 so that his little boy could see where his grandfather had worked years before. All at once, Leonard shouted, "Look! There's someone in the furnace!" John slowed down for a better look and caught a glimpse of a man strolling through the sparks. At that moment, John remembered the words that his father had told his mother years before: "As long as there's a furnace standing in the county, I'll be there."

LUCAS TAVERN, MONTGOMERY

Today, the word "tavern" is used simply to mean "bar"—an establishment where adults can buy and drink alcoholic drinks. In the 1800s, however, taverns were small hotels where weary travelers could spend the night and get a hot meal. One of the most popular Alabama taverns of that time opened in 1818 on Federal Road, just west of Line Creek in Montgomery. In 1821 the original owner, James Abercrombie, sold the tavern to Walter B. Lucas. Under his ownership, the business became known as Lucas Tavern and was a popular overnight stop. Guests were greeted at the door by Walter's daughter, Eliza, and were served ham, chicken, vegetables, and preserved fruit. Even famous visitors like the Marquis de Lafayette, a French aristocrat who fought alongside American colonists against the British in the American Revolution, came to stay while the Lucas family ran the tavern.

By the 1840s, the tavern had become a private residence, but it was later abandoned. The Landmarks Foundation purchased Lucas Tavern in 1978 and had it moved to a historic neighborhood called Old Alabama Town, where it remains to this day. Not only is it the oldest standing building in Montgomery County . . . but one of the most haunted.

The hauntings at Lucas Tavern began in 1980, after the historic building was restored and reopened as a working restaurant. Visitors reported seeing the figure of a five-foot-three-inch woman in her twenties, waving at them from a window or doorway. The tavern's resident ghost was said to be the spirit of Eliza Lucas, who seemed to be a friendly, welcoming spirit from the past.

However, toward the end of the 1980s, Eliza's angry side began to emerge. One afternoon, as a group of men held a committee meeting in the tavern, a loud disagreement broke out. One irate man stood up from the table and walked over to the front of the building. He was shaking his fist at the committee and calling some of the members names when, all at once, smoke belched from the fireplace, covering the man in soot.

On another occasion, two staff members were sitting at a table in the tavern, complaining about the way Old Alabama Town was being run, when suddenly, the front door fell off its hinges and crashed to the floor. Because no logical explanation for either of these strange occurrences could be found, the people of Old Alabama Town blamed Eliza Lucas's ghost for both paranormal disturbances. One suspects that when Eliza was alive and working for her father, she might have been charged with keeping the peace in the tavern, just as she does now.

Old Bryce Hospital, Tuscaloosa

In the 18th and 19th centuries, mental hospitals were not much better than prisons. Tuscaloosa's Bryce Hospital, which opened in 1859, was meant to be different—at least in the beginning. The hospital was named for its first superintendent, Peter Bryce, who was hired because of his reformist ideas. He replaced the shackles and straightjackets used in most mental hospitals with kindness, respect, and understanding. Under his direction, patients were taught useful skills like sewing. The hospital even had its own dairy, laundry, and newspaper.

In the 20th century, however, the budget was cut, and the quality of patient care for Bryce's 5,200 patients declined. The hospital received national attention for the 1971 court case involving

Ricky Wyatt, a fifteen-year-old boy with no signs of mental illness who was confined to the now run-down facility. News coverage revealed the terrible conditions, including the fact that many slept on filthy mattresses while others slept on the floor. In 2009, the patients were moved to a newly constructed facility on McFarland Boulevard. The University of Alabama purchased Bryce Hospital in 2010 for close to ninety million dollars, intending to convert it into the Performing Arts Academic Center.

Reports of hauntings began at the Jemison Center, also known as Old Bryce Hospital, which was separate from the main building.

It was built as a satellite hospital seven miles away to relieve pressure on the newer, central Hospital. Old Bryce Hospital had stood abandoned since it was closed in 1977, though it was often visited by curious trespassers eager to see if there was any truth in the ghostly activity they had heard about: sounds of running footsteps in empty hallways, the ringing of disconnected telephones,

maniacal laughter, voices coming through the disconnected intercom, and the scraping of chairs on the floors of empty rooms. Many trespassers swore that cold spots could be found throughout the hospital. A few people even claimed they had been scratched by unseen hands.

The historic hospital's best-known ghost story involves the spirit of a little boy around eight years old. Legend has it that a boy of that age died during hydrotherapy—a treatment where the patient is immersed in a vat of water. The ghost of a little blonde-haired boy wearing suspenders has been sighted many times in the main building. Some of the soft-hearted visitors to the old hospital have left toys for him to play with.

Many researchers into the paranormal believe that suffering has a way of imprinting itself on the landscape of old battlefields and on the floors and walls of old prisons and hospitals. This explanation could account for the sights and sounds that periodically replay in Old Bryce Hospital.

THE PICKENS COUNTY COURTHOUSE, CARROLLTON

On April 5, 1865, Union soldiers under the command of General John T. Croxton burned down the Pickens County Courthouse, even though the building was not of any value to the Union Army. Over the next few years, the citizens of Carrollton pooled together their time and resources and erected a fine wooden building to replace it. To them, the new structure represented a restoration of law and order. So they were infuriated when, on November 17, 1876, the courthouse burned down again! The people of Carrollton demanded that the sheriff make an arrest. The

Pickens County Courthouse

sheriff didn't have any real suspects, but under pressure, he pinned the crime on a former slave named Henry Wells. Wells learned that the sheriff was looking for him and dropped out of sight for two years. But when his grandmother lay dying, Wells risked coming out of hiding to visit her . . . and was arrested on the spot.

The sheriff imprisoned Henry in the attic of the newly rebuilt courthouse. Around midnight, while storm clouds were forming in the sky, a crowd of angry men formed on the lawn outside the courthouse. The story goes that when Henry looked out of the window, he noticed a jug of whiskey was being passed around, and one of the members of the mob was holding a rope. The crowd was out of control and looked ready to murder. As lightning flashed across the sky, Henry's fear turned into anger, and he exclaimed, "I am innocent! If you kill me, I will haunt you for the rest of your lives!" Of course, the crowd couldn't hear his warning, but it probably would not have made any difference if they had. Several of the men dashed up the stairs, dragged Henry out of the courthouse, and transported him to the swamp outside of town, where they hung him from an oak tree.

Early the next morning, one of the men who had killed Henry Wells was walking past the courthouse when he noticed a face staring

down at him. At first, he blamed the corn whiskey he had been drinking the night before for the hallucination. He rubbed his eyes and looked again: The face was still there! The man began running around town, yelling for the townspeople to look at the face that seemed etched into the window. Several attempts were made to remove the image with wire brushes, soap, and water, but it always returned. Apparently, in the 1920s, a severe hailstorm broke every window in the courthouse except the one with Henry's face.

Today, you can look through the telescope mounted across the street and see the face in the window. A wooden arrow points to the image, which some say resembles a smiley face. Maybe Henry has reason to smile, since no one who has seen the window has been able to forget it—or the murder that took place on that dark and stormy night.

THE TALLASSEE PUBLIC LIBRARY, TALLASSEE

When you visit the library, there are certain items you expect to find. Lots and lots of books, for one thing. Probably a handful of copy machines and computers, too. There are often community gardens and telescopes at the library. Not to mention the occasional stern librarian. But did you know you can sometimes find *ghosts* at the library? For years, most of Tallassee Library's patrons have been well acquainted with the wide variety of services offered by the library. No one realized that the possibility of having a paranormal experience was one of them until 1999.

Perhaps not surprisingly, the first active spirits in the library were the ghosts of children. Librarian Sharon

Kilpatrick said that when she opened the library every morning, the first sound she heard was laughter and the patter of little feet in the Children's Room. She was never really frightened until the day she saw two people—a young man and a small child, holding hands—walk into the Children's Room, enter the stacks, and vanish.

On another occasion, Sharon was walking past the opened door of the toy-storage closet in the Children's Room and spotted a rocking horse rocking by itself. A minute or so later, a little boy around three years old stopped at  the entrance to the empty Children's Room, telling his mother he did not want to go inside because he didn't know the two little boys playing there.

Most librarians have a strong commitment to their library and the people who use it. For Tallassee Library's very first librarian, Mary Lou Martin, that dedication seems to have lasted beyond the grave. Mary Lou worked as Tallassee's librarian for twenty-six years, starting in 1922, and her service is memorialized with a portrait that hangs in the library. Though she was important to the library's beginning, she was known during her life as a "cold" person. Apparently, she still is, even after death! "Several of our patrons have experienced cold chills and fear so strong that their hearts feel like they are coming out of their chests while in the room with her portrait," Sharon said. There have been times when Sharon, too, wanted to get out of that room as fast as she could.

Strange sounds echo through the building as well. Early in the morning or late in the evening, when the librarians are all alone, they have heard loud crashing sounds coming from the stacks. Thinking that one of the large shelves has fallen over, they run upstairs, only to find that nothing is out of order. The sounds of people talking together have been heard downstairs in the book sale room. "It sounds like everyday people," Sharon said. "They're not trying to be quiet. By the time you get to the bottom of the steps, it's gone."

If you visit the Tallassee Public Library looking for a good story, beware: Some spooky stories might be looking for you, too!

Haunted Outdoors

THE BOYINGTON OAK, MOBILE

Charles Boyington arrived in Mobile, Alabama in 1933, on the same day a meteor shower made it look like "stars fell on Alabama." Many people viewed the event as sign of bad luck. For Charles, though, it was the beginning of a string of good things ... at least in the beginning. Within a few days of his arrival, he was hired by the printing firm of Pollard and Dale. He also found a place to stay at Mrs. George's boarding house, with a quiet roommate named Nathaniel Frost, who was soon a good friend. After a couple of months, Charles fell in love with the beautiful Rose Le Fleur. For a while, the future looked bright.

The following spring, Charles's luck seemed to turn. First, he lost his job. As a result, he couldn't marry Rose. He left town in despair. And then came the biggest blow of all: His roommate, Nathaniel, was found stabbed to death in Church Street Graveyard ... and Charles, whose departure raised suspicion, was charged with the crime. He was taken back to Mobile, where he was tried and found guilty of murder. The judge sentenced him to be hanged on February 20, 1835.

On the day of his execution, Charles had to walk behind his coffin as hundreds of spectators looked on. When they reached Washington Square, a minister spoke with Charles, offering words of comfort, while the sheriff stood aside with a friend. All of a sudden, the sheriff, his friend, and the sheriff's horse fell into a dead faint. They recovered a few seconds later, but eyewitnesses took this strange event as a bad omen.

Charles then walked up the steps to the gallows, where the hangman placed the noose around his neck. Charles turned to the crowd and declared that a huge oak tree would grow from his grave as proof of his innocence. Following his hanging, his body was taken to the Church Street Graveyard and buried in the potter's field—a section with unmarked graves for those who could not afford private burial. People checked on his grave periodically to see if Charles's prediction had come true. Then one day, a tiny sprout poked its head through the dirt where Charles's body lay. The seedling eventually developed into a massive oak tree. The potter's field is now a parking lot, but the tree still stands: a living monument in place of a tombstone.

CRY BABY HOLLOW, HARTSELLE

Lonely, out-of-the-way places in the woods or the countryside have always been popular hangouts for young people. Old abandoned buildings, train tunnels, graveyards, and other spooky places draw thrill seekers and "Legend Trippers," determined to prove their courage or give their friends a good old-fashioned scare. In Hartselle, Cry Baby Hollow is just this type of place.

Locals say that the hollow and the one-lane concrete bridge spanning the creek are

haunted by the ghost of a baby who died there many years ago. In one telling from the 1800s, a Cherokee woman was picking nuts and berries in the hollow, carrying her baby on her back in a mortar board. Suddenly, storm clouds darkened the sky, and torrents of water surged through the hollow, washing the woman away. She survived, but her baby was never found. In the 1940s, another baby was lost in the creek alongside its mother, when a murderer killed and disposed of the pair in that very spot. In the most recent version, a troubled girl threw her own infant off the bridge into the creek.

Some people who have walked through Cry Baby Hollow at night claim to have heard the crying of a baby echoing through the trees. Others swear that if you park on the bridge and leave a candy bar on the rear bumper, teeth marks will appear on the treat! Not content to wait to leave the haunting up to fate, some admit to hiding under the bridge to cry out at passing cars. One Hartselle resident even has a recording of a baby crying to spook her passengers as she drives over the bridge!

The Harrison Cemetery, Coffee County

Grancer Harrison moved his family from South Carolina to Coffee County, Alabama, in the 1830s. Like many planters who came to Alabama at that time, he was lured by the state's rich, black soil. He purchased a large farm, planted corn and cotton, and soon became one of the most successful planters in the entire county. Although he was immensely proud of his "planter's hands," Grancer's first love was socializing. Every Saturday night, his neighbors flocked to his plantation for barbecues and horse races. His dances, held in the huge dance hall he designed himself, were the big draw. It was said that mid-way through the evening, Grancer would step out onto the waxed dance floor wearing his dancing shoes and specially made dancing clothes, and perform the Buck Dance, much to the delight of the admiring crowd.

Grancer continued to hold dances on his property up to the very end. When he was on his deathbed, he told his family, "When I die, I want to be dressed in my dancing clothes, and I want my dancing shoes placed on my feet, and I want to be laid out on my featherbed. Then tell the pallbearers to carry the bed inside the tomb." His last wishes were carried out to the letter.

Not long after Grancer was placed inside his tomb—bed and all— in the Harrison Cemetery, people

passing by claimed to have heard the clomping of dancing feet and the melodious strains of traditional fiddle tunes. Sometimes, a booming male voice could be heard calling out square dances. The large, wooden grave shelter has long since rotted away, and his tomb has been vandalized and rebuilt. However, according to locals, Grancer Harrison's love of dancing seems to have outlasted death itself.

THE TOMBIGBEE RIVER, PENNINGTON

In the 1850s, steamboats carried freight and passengers up and down the Tombigbee River ... and accidents were common. Steamboats occasionally sideswiped each other, but the damage was usually minimal. Submerged logs presented more of a problem because a steamboat could sink if one of these hidden hazards gouged a hole in the bottom of the vessel. Boiler explosions were the biggest cause of death on the Tombigbee. However, in late February 1858, a sidewheel steamboat called the *Eliza Battle* fell victim to an entirely different type of threat.

What turned out to be the *Eliza Battle's* last voyage was promoted in the newspapers as a gala event. The owners encouraged the families of planters to combine business with pleasure by accompanying their bales of cotton down to

New Orleans. Wearing little hats and holding parasols, the ladies boarded the boat in their finest dresses. The ship was decorated with colorful banners and Japanese lanterns. Two bands and a calliope entertained passengers. As night fell, snow and sleet coated the decks. But suddenly, shouts of "Fire!" drowned out the jubilant sounds of music and laughter. To passengers' horror, flames had spread from the cotton bales to the engine room, cabins, and gangways. People scrambled to gather their family members before abandoning the ship.

Passengers dived overboard into the freezing water. In the water, people climbed on top of floating cotton bales and pieces of floating lumber. Many clung to the overhanging branches of the trees lining the river.

The screams alerted the citizens of nearby Naheola. By morning, a crowd of locals had created makeshift rafts and were trying to pluck survivors out of the trees and water. James Eckridge, a resident of Naheola, picked up around one hundred people and carried them to shore in his little boat. Eighteen-year-old

Frank Stone, who had worked on the *Eliza Battle* as second clerk, dived into the icy river and rescued the young son of Mr. and Mrs. Bat Cromwell. He dived into the river once again and placed Miss Turner on top of a cotton bale but was unable to save any of her family members. Many more would have perished that night had it not been for Rebecca Coleman Pettigrew, who turned her large home into a hospital for the survivors and provided huge cauldrons of soup all night long.

No one knows for sure how many people died that night. Estimates range from twenty-nine to one hundred twenty. The cause of the fire is also unknown, although some historians believe that sparks from the Japanese lanterns could have set the cotton bales ablaze. Divers later located the rotting remains of the *Eliza Battle* in twenty-eight feet of water, not far from Pennington. But some say the *Eliza Battle* rises again each February: floating eerily on the Tombigbee on the anniversary of the disaster, continuing its journey on the wintry river.

HUGGIN' MOLLY, ABBEVILLE

Cautionary tales are scary stories meant to encourage good behavior. Some feature mythic creatures like the "Sack Man," who gathers disobedient children in a big bag and carries them off, or the "Bogeyman," who is similarly out to get naughty kids. From Haiti to Asia, parents warn children of the weird and wild bad guys waiting to give rule-breakers their due. In Abbeville, Alabama, a female version of this punishing phantom has been scaring children for many years.

Stories of Huggin' Molly first surfaced in the early 20th century. She was a seven-foot-tall phantom "as big around as a bale of cotton." She followed unruly children walking around

Abbeville after sundown and crushed them in her strong embrace. Some adults told their children and grandchildren that Huggin' Molly would grab them if they were out after curfew and scream in their ears. Schoolchildren claimed that she lived in a dark alley behind the schoolhouse. At least one older man told his grandchildren that he himself barely escaped being hugged to death late one night.

Abbeville resident Mack Taylor is certain he met Huggin' Molly as a teenager, when he had an after-school job in a grocery store. One evening, just as it was starting to get dark— and as he was finishing up a neighborhood grocery delivery— Mack sensed someone walking behind him. He spun around and was shocked to see a black-robed female figure walking his way. Fueled by fear, Mack began running as fast as he could toward home. He bounded up the front steps and slammed the door behind him.

Like many towns with local legends, Abbeville has made the most of its famed phantom. Visitors driving into town are greeted by a welcome sign featuring a witch-like woman chasing a little boy. And if you want to hear more stories about Huggin' Molly, you can sample the local cuisine and an earful of scary stories at a local restaurant named—what else?—but "Huggin' Molly's."

A Ghostly Goodbye

You may still be on the fence about whether or not you believe in ghosts. But if you're searching for evidence that ghosts are real, Alabama has *plenty*. With its centuries of history—some of it very dark, indeed—there's simply no shortage of spookiness. From its antebellum mansions and battlefields to its historic universities, eerie taverns, creepy cemeteries, and abandoned hospitals, it's no wonder ghost hunters and paranormal researchers alike love exploring Alabama. So if you're feeling brave and in the mood for something spooky, grab your flashlight . . . and join them.

Alan Brown teaches English at the University of West Alabama in Livingston, Alabama. Alan has written primarily about southern ghost lore, a passion that has taken him to haunted places throughout the entire Deep South, as well as parts of the Midwest and the Southwest. Alan's wife, Marilyn, accompanies him on these trips and occasionally serves as his "ghost magnet." Her encounters with the spirit world have been incorporated in a number of Alan's books. In 2018, Alan decided to explore another abiding interest of his—mysteries and legends—in books like *Eerie Alabama* and *The Unexplained South*. Alan wrote this book with encouragement—and input—from his grandsons, Cade and Owen.

Check out some of the other *Spooky America* titles available now!

Spooky America was adapted from the creeptastic *Haunted America* series for adults. *Haunted America* explores historical haunts in cities and regions across America. Here's more from the original *Haunted Alabama* author Alan Brown: